> POETRY IS NOT THE RHYME
> IT IS THE HEART
> SPEAKING IN THE GAPS
> AND DARKNESS
> AND QUIET
> AND FROM LONELY THINGS
> THAT TALK

Mazuri Press
Mazuri@Fadum.com
United States of America
This book is a work of poetry
and painting by Morten E. Fadum
Images are of the authors
imagination or of antiquity

Mazuri Press is the registered
trademark of Fadum Studio
Designed by Morten E. Fadum
Printed and bound by
Worzalla Publishing Co.
Stevens Point, Wisconsin, U.S.A.

ISBN 9651148-1-3

Also by
Morten E. Fadum

EVEN POETS DANCE

Original art by Morten E. Fadum
available....contact
Morten@Fadum.com

A
WHISPERING
IN
THE
LEAVES

BY

MORTEN
FADUM

FOR
PATTI

I'VE LIVED WITH YOU
THESE THOUSAND YEARS
SOMETIMES IN CASTLES
MADE OF SAND

WE'VE SHARED ALL THINGS
THAT LOVERS SHARE
SOME SURPRISE
SOME THINGS WE PLANNED

WE'VE DANCED OUR LIFE
IN MANY WAYS
BUT WE'VE DANCED OUR LIFE
TOGETHER

I KNOW ONLY THE DANCER STOPS
BUT THE DANCE
GOES ON
FOREVER

AND THE TURTLE SAID
ALL
THAT YOU SEEK
IS IN YOU

READING THE THUNDER
AND THE RUSTLING
OF LEAVES

I AM A TRAVELER
SEARCHING
A GREAT
MYSTERY

AT THE HEARTH
   WITH MORNING COALS
LAY FRAGRANT WOOD
   TO CAST A FIRE GLOW
      OF WARMTH
      AND CRACKLED SONG

   TO START THE DAY
      TO HEAT PORRIGE AND COFFEE
AND WARM AWAY THE COLD
      BAKE BREAD
      FROM SHOVELLED EMBERS
SIMMER SOUP
      FOR LATE TONIGHT
KEEP THIS ANCIENT CABIN WARM
      HOME BY EVENING
      TO BANK THE FIRE
      BEFORE I SLEEP
AND WAKE TO WARMTH AGAIN

ONLY THE DANCER STOPS
AND THE DANCE
GOES ON FOREVER

If your Heart
must break

Let it
Break
Open

BREAKING WAVES
AND TOO BLUE SEA

REFLECTIONS
OF MORNING LIGHT

SHARE WITH ME
YOUR SECRET DREAMS
I WANT TO SLEEP WITH YOU TONIGHT

SHE

IS A LEADER

IN ALL THINGS

... BUT
WHEN
SHE WAS YOUNG

SHE WAS SUCH
A WILD
GIRL

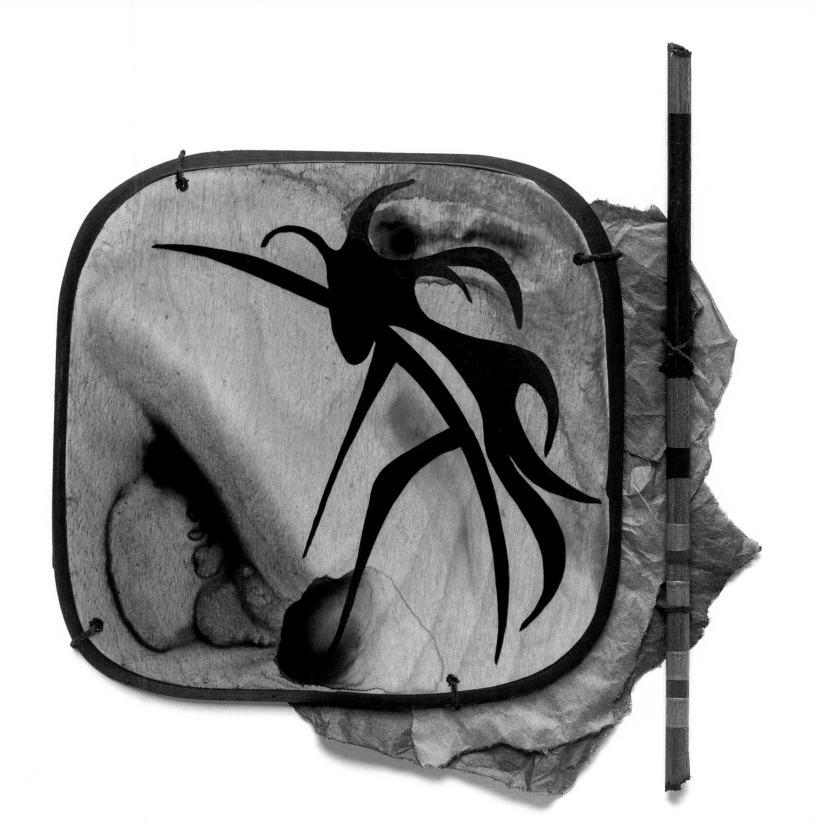

WE
ARE A SERIES
OF SMALL
COINCIDENCES

The Water Walkers
Make Silent Whispers
On A Quiet Sea

Dancers Over Sleeping Oceans
Runners Before The Mist
Hiders From The Morning Light
Messengers From Ancient Souls

The Water Walkers
The Tides Are Their Breathing
The Breeze Is Their Blood
Searchers
For The New Heart Beating

The Waterwalkers

DRIVEN
BY ANCIENT
CODE

THROUGH WHITE FOAM
LIKE CLOUDS

UP WATERS FALL
AND AIR

FROZEN IN MIST
AND TIME

KICK HARD
SILVER SISTER

PUSH ON
TIRED BROTHER

SOON TO BE HOME AGAIN

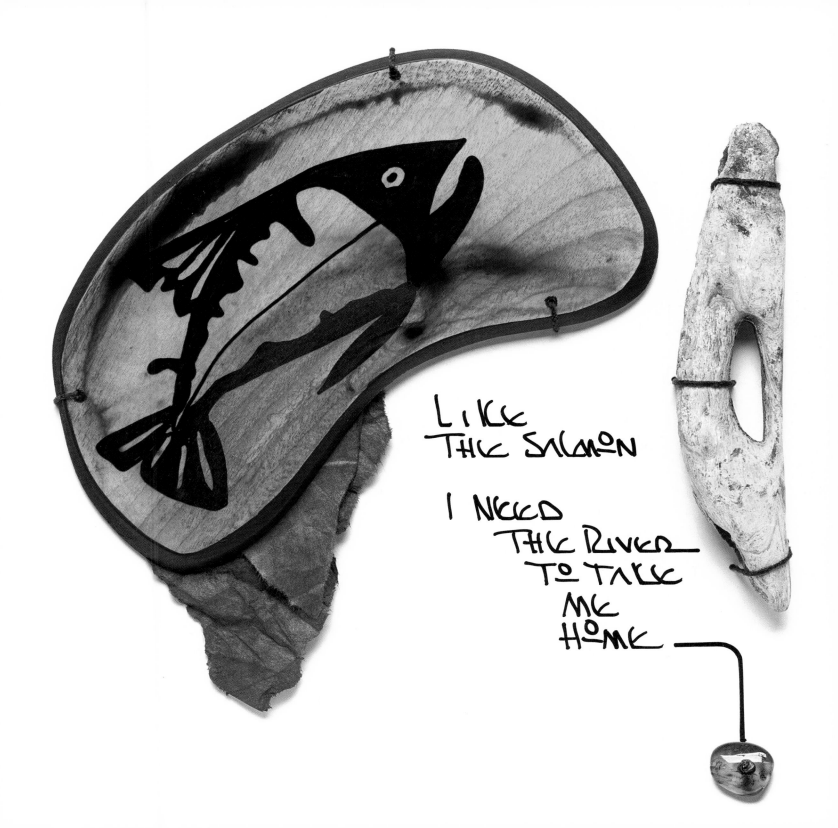

LIKE
THE SALMON

I NEED
THE RIVER
TO TAKE
ME
HOME

THE WINDS
BLEW THE ASHES
INTO THE HILLS

AND THE SAND
HAS COVERED
THE SCARS

ONLY THE HORSES
ARE LEFT TO PLAY
UNDER
THE MIDNIGHT
STARS

ON THE RIVER
AND OUT
OF THE MIST

WE GAVE DEATH
AND DANCING
EQUAL PLACE

NO ONE
ASKED FOR LESS

IT
WAS A GREAT
ADVENTURE

GATHERING BASKET OF BRITTLE
STICK... WOVE WITH NIMBLE CARE
STAINED by BERRY AND GARDEN
TREASURE...BITS of fur from
WINTER GAME... CHIPS of FIREWOOD

YOU ARE AN ANCIENT THING...
    YOUR STORY IN THE WEAVE
    YOUR OWNERS PAST

YOU'VE LIVED A HUMANS Life
feed YOUR NEIGHBORS
WHEN THERE WAS NEED

YOU'RE VERY OLD... YOUR TWIGS
GONE DRY... NO MORE TASKS TO
SERVE

LET ME TAKE YOU FROM THIS
GLOOM...TO THE WOOD...RELEASE
YOU TO THE forest floor...
TO RISE AS VINE AGAIN

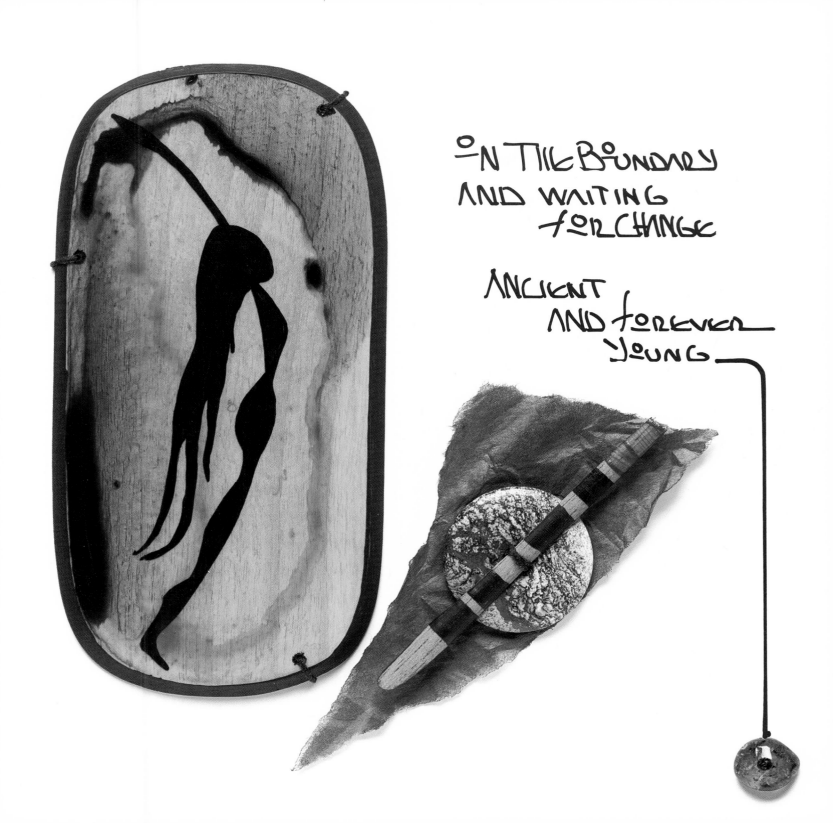

ON THE BOUNDARY
AND WAITING
    FOR CHANGE

ANCIENT
    AND FOREVER
        YOUNG

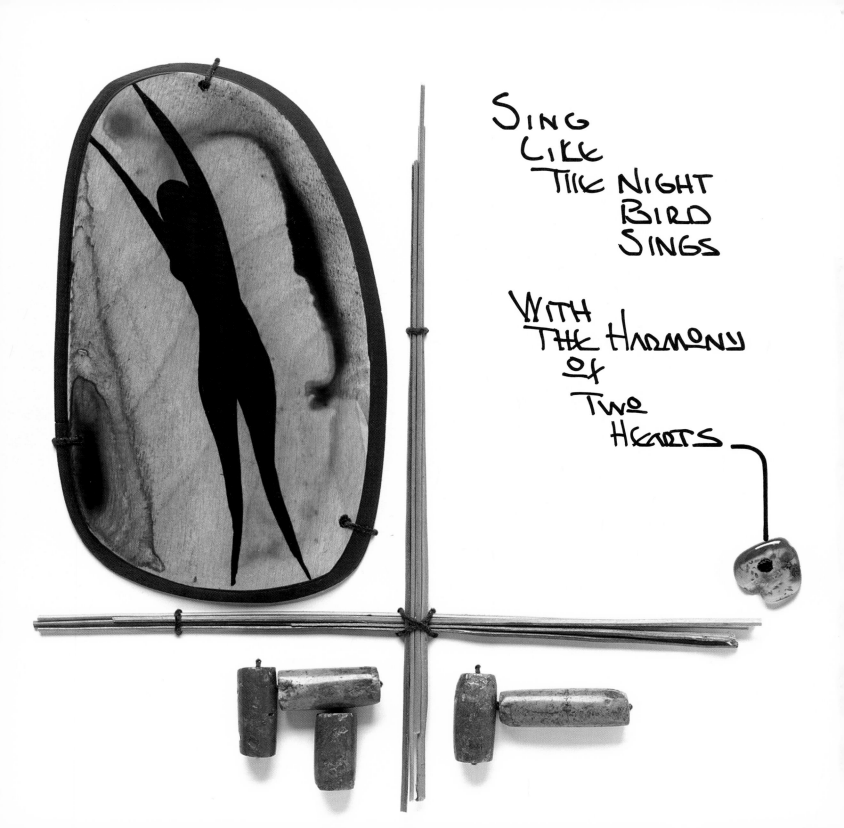

SING
LIKE
THE NIGHT
BIRD
SINGS

WITH
THE HARMONY
OF
TWO
HEARTS

She carried me
from the jungle
Set me gently by the sea
The tides came in
The water cool
She washed the dirt from me

...But jungle vines
Like gentle hands
Stay wrapped
Around my spine
And I turn
To take the jungle in
And wonder
What
I'll find

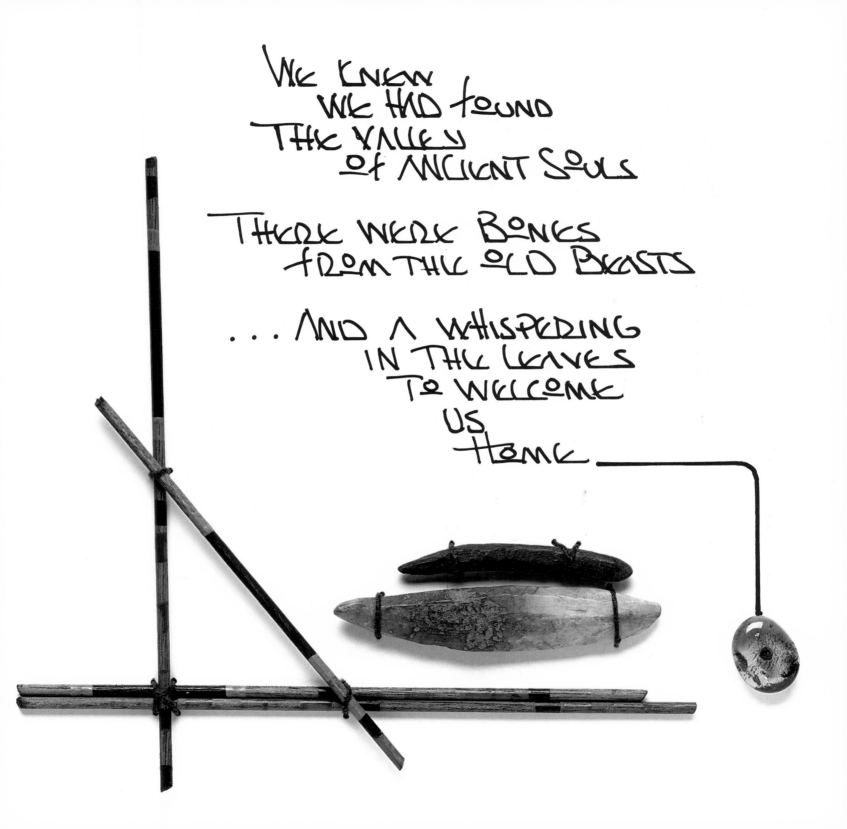

WE KNEW
WE HAD found
THE VALLEY
of ANCIENT SOULS

THERE WERE BONES
FROM THE OLD BEASTS

... AND A WHISPERING
IN THE LEAVES
TO WELCOME
US
HOME

THERE IS
A STRUGGLE
IN ALL
OF US

THIS IS THE WAY
IT HAS ALWAYS
BEEN

THE WOLFING WAYS
LAY TIRED AND LONG
    YOURS IS THE KILL

THE WOLFING WAYS
    WALK AT FOREST EDGE
HEARING WHAT NO ONE HEARS

THE WOLFING WAYS
    MY CHILD'S DEN
    WITH HUNTERS PAW
        AT MOON LIGHT

THE WOLFING WAYS
    MY PREDATORS HEART
BEATS ONE MILLION YEARS

THE WOLFING WAYS

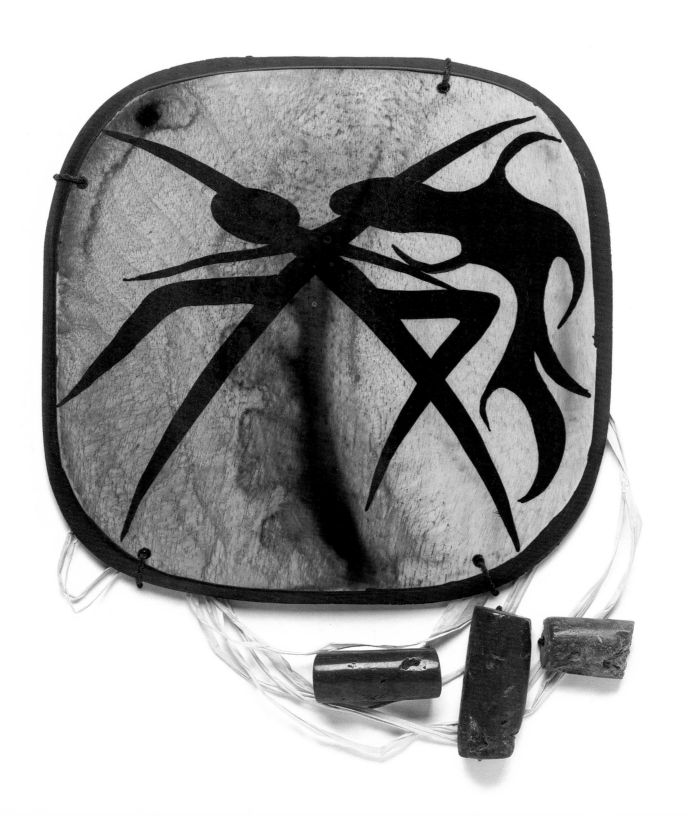

IN THE WHIRLWIND
THERE WAS A SONG
THIS SONG WAS A WOMAN
 AND THIS SONG
 WAS THE SMELL OF EARTH
 AND THIS SONG
 WAS TO HOLD A CHILD

DANCE THE WHIRLWIND DANCE
 AND NO HEART
 REMAIN HEAVY
 AND NO HEART
 WILL STAY
 LOST

Dancing with your Shadow
in a small fire Light

Dancing with your Shadow
Till the moon Gets Bright

Dancing with your Shadow
and Beating on a Drum

Dancing with your Shadow
Till the sun Light comes

EVEN
POETS
DANCE

The fog
    Takes its rolling step
Damp foot
    On surface smooth
It halts the human journey
It wakes the primitive soul

In it is the essence
    of all it touches
    A taste of pine
The richness
    of the forest floor
The laughter of children
The lingerers in empty places

    Breath it deeply
        this fogged air
Suck it far into your soul

        ...it will shiver your
            memory

I AM HER LOVER

SHE

IS MY DANCER

WE

ARE THE KEEPERS

OF

^ HEART

I HAVE A WOODEN BOAT
AND SAIL
THAT GLIDES ACROSS A SEA
OF SILVER FISH
AND GENTLE WAVES
THAT ROCK ME IN MY DREAMS

I'M BACK IN TIME
A THOUSAND YEARS
SAILING TO A SHORE
TO FIND A PLACE
THAT NO ONE'S SEEN
WHERE NO ONE'S BEEN BEFORE

I DROP THE SAIL
AND DRIFT IN CLOSE
STEP OUT UPON THE SAND
BUT HAPPY
WITH THE SIMPLE TRUTH
I'M BACK WHERE I BEGAN

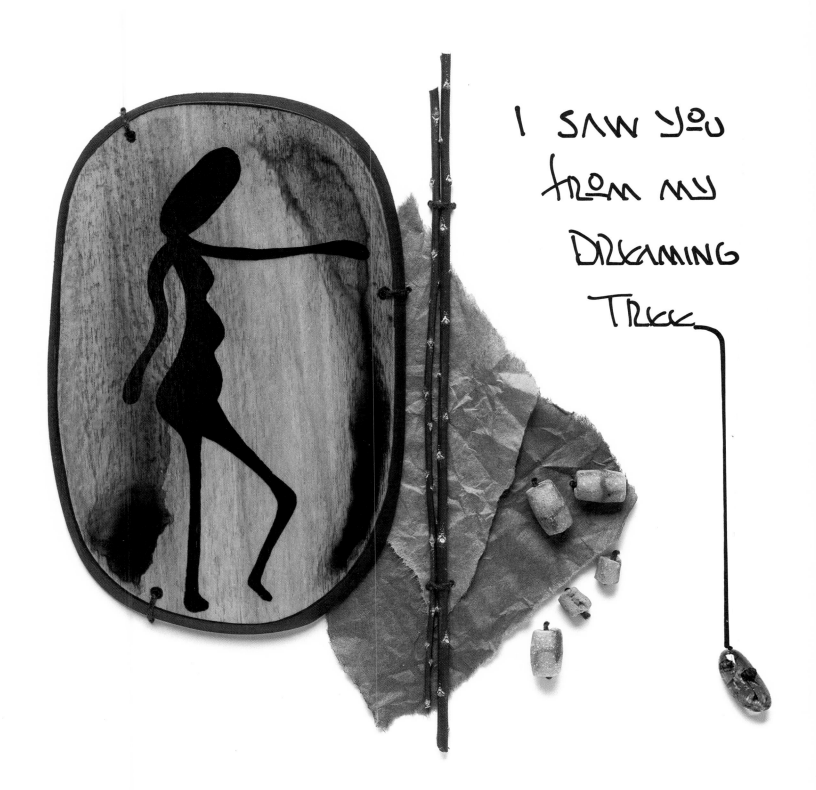

I SAW YOU from my DREAMING TREEE

WHILE WALKING IN MOON GLOW
STEP ONLY IN LIGHT
WHEN MOON GLOWS ARE GLOWING
THEY HOLD BACK THE NIGHT

DON'T FEAR TO TOUCH THEM
THEY'RE SOFTER THAN AIR
THE GLOW OF THE MOON GLOW
THE NOTHING
THAT'S THERE
THE LIGHT AND THE FEELING
IS A GIFT
JUST FOR YOU
AND AFTER THE MOON GLOW
THE SUN WILL SHINE THROUGH
BUT WAIT FOR THE NEXT TIME
MORE WONDERS TO SEE
WHEN MOON GLOWS ARE GLOWING
WHEN MOON GLOWS ARE GLOWING
WHEN MOON GLOWS ARE GLOWING
FOR MY CHILD AND ME_____